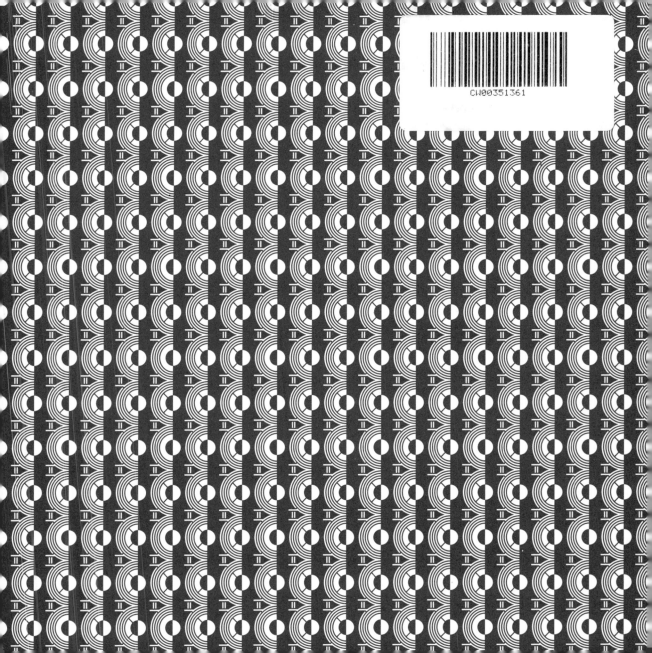

CW00351361

DUMBBELLS
EAR CAPS AND
HAIR RESTORERS

A REMARKABLE INVENTION FOR THE CULTURE OF HAIR

THE EVANS VACUUM CAP is a practical invention, constructed on scientific and hygienic principles, by the simple means of which a free and normal circulation is restored throughout the scalp. The minute blood vessels are gently stimulated to activity, thus allowing the food supply, which can only be derived from the blood, to be carried to the hair roots, the effects of which are quickly seen in a healthy, vigorous growth of hair. There is no rubbing, and as no drugs or chemicals of whatsoever kind are employed there is nothing to cause irritation. It is only necessary to wear the Cap three or four minutes daily.

THE COMPANY'S GUARANTEE.

An EVANS VACUUM CAP will be sent you for sixty days' free trial. If you do not see a gradual development of a new growth of hair, and are not convinced that the Cap will completely restore your hair, you are at liberty to return the Cap with no expense whatever to yourself. It is requested, as an evidence of good faith, that the price of the Cap be deposited with the Chancery Lane Safe Deposit Company, of London, the largest financial and business institution of the kind in the world, who will issue a receipt, guaranteeing that the money will be returned in full, on demand, without questions or comment, at any time during the trial period.

The eminent Dr. I. N. LOVE, in his address to the Medical Board on the subject of Alopæcia (loss of hair), stated **that if a means could be devised to bring nutrition to the hair follicles (hair roots) without resorting to any irritating process, the problem of hair growth would be solved.** Later on, when the EVANS VACUUM CAP was submitted to him for inspection, **he remarked that the Cap would fulfil and confirm in practice the observations he had previously made before the Medical Board.**

Dr. W. MOORE, referring to the invention, said that the **principle upon which the Evans Vacuum Cap is founded is absolutely correct and indisputable.**

An Illustrated and Descriptive Book of the Evans Vacuum Cap will be sent post free on application.

THE MANAGER EVANS VACUUM CAP CO., Ltd.,
REGENT HOUSE, REGENT STREET, LONDON, W.

DUMBBELLS EAR CAPS AND HAIR RESTORERS

A Shopper's Guide to Gentlemen's Foibles 1800s–1930s

Jane Furnival

Michael O'Mara Books Limited

Dedicated to All Men Who Need Encouragement

———————————

First published in Great Britain in 1999 by
Michael O'Mara Books Limited
9 Lion Yard, Tremadoc Road
London SW4 7NQ

A CIP catalogue record for this book
is available from the British Library

ISBN 1-85479-464-7

1 3 5 7 9 10 8 6 4 2

Designed and typeset by Martin Bristow

Printed and bound in Singapore by Tien Wah Press

CONTENTS

Introduction 6

The Well-Groomed Gentleman 8

The Properly-Attired Gentleman 24

The Gentleman at Home 42

The Gentleman at Leisure 48

The Gentleman at Large 54

Acknowledgements 64

INTRODUCTION

If you can keep your head when all about you are losing theirs, you'll be a man. But to be a gentleman, you need a huge array of clothes and equipment.

Here is your guide to the kit a chap needs. It has everything from dumbbells to dinners, including devices to make moustaches stick out, ears stick in and more.

It enlightens you on tiny but telling points of etiquette, like why a fellow never lets a

lady choose his tie and how to insult someone using your top hat. It gets you out and about to exclusive clubs and fashionable haunts, hunting, shooting and fishing in the country, and driving your new car in goggles specially adapted to spot a speed policeman 'even if posing as a respectable man'.

Ironically, perhaps, gentlemen do not 'go shopping', unless for some trinket for a lady (or not-quite-a-lady – which is more fun). They don't buy things; they acquire possessions, preferably by the dozen. Nothing must look new. Your valet must 'wear in' your trousers; your driver wear your jacket out in the rain to achieve a well-used effect.

A purchase must last. Rather than replacing it (a bore), it is sent for repair. Generosity in large matters is gentlemanly, but such small economies are personal triumphs.

BALDNESS
IS NOT
NATURAL !

BEFORE USING.   AFTER USING.

Nature will restore the Hair if you will help it, even as a worn-out soil will grow good crops if you feed it with a proper fertilizer. If a farmer was to apply lime where stable manure was needed, and failed to get a crop, was it the fault of the soil or of knowledge on his part? If we have hitherto worked from a wrong principle and failed, is it any reason why success should not be reached? BENTON'S HAIR GROWER will **GROW HAIR, CURE DANDRUFF, and STOP FALLING HAIR.** Price, $1.00 per Bottle, by mail free.

Address, **BENTON HAIR GROWER CO., Brainard Block, Cleveland, O.**

THE WELL-GROOMED GENTLEMAN

A Fine Head of Hair

Luxuriant facial hair is the ticket to social success. Our gallant naval officers do not ask permission to grow a beard, only to shave it off. Never employ a hirsute butler, however. Many are so well-dressed that a clean-shaven appearance is the only way to ensure that visitors do not mistake butlers for chaps like ourselves.

If his hair preys on his mind, a gentleman may purchase a patent preparation, perhaps a Red Indian remedy with bear's grease, guaranteed to produce an instant crown of hair, silky whiskers and extravagant

eyebrows. The most efficacious cures stop grey hair and headaches too.

Science has produced many hair-restoring machines. The 'Evans Vacuum Cap', worn four minutes daily in the privacy of your dressing-room, stimulates the bloodflow to the follicles. Deposit the cost with Chancery Lane Safe Deposit Company and ask for it back if not completely satisfied.

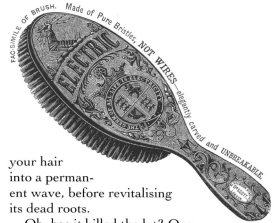

Dr Scott's 'Electric Hair Brush' soothes the weary brain whilst husbanding hair-growth. The Lektrik electric comb shocks your hair into a perman-ent wave, before revitalising its dead roots.

Oh, has it killed the lot? One and a half guineas buys Ross & Son's 'Invisible Ventilating Head of Hair'. A wig? Never! A veritable work of art.

THE INVISIBLE VENTILATING HEADS OF HAIR.

ROSS & SON'S METHOD OF MEASURING THE HEAD.

	Inches.	Eighths.
The Round of the Head		
From Ear to Ear		
From Forehead to Poll.....		

These inimitable works of art, for both Ladies and Gentlemen, from One Guinea-and-a-half upwards.

THE ATRAPILATORY, OR LIQUID HAIR DYE, the only Dye that really answers for all colours. Ross & Sons can recommend the above Dye as infallible.

Training the Moustache

Beards signify authority, but moustachios
are the height of virility. Once grown,
moustachios should be combed, dyed if
necessary, with 'Imperial Hair Dye' (which
arrives privately packed), then tortured into
exquisite points, fixed and beautified with
'Carter's Threxaline'.

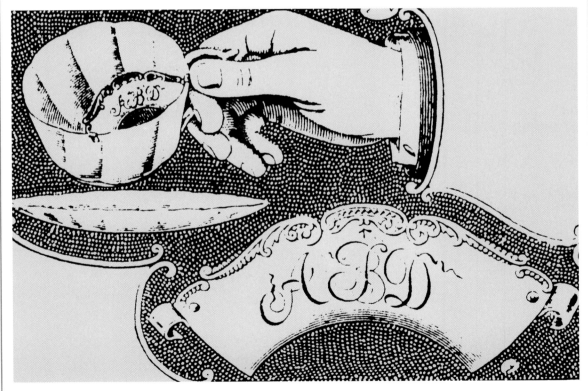

Regularly wax and nourish your moustachios with macassar oil.

Prevent drink from wilting or food from lodging in your moustachios by strapping on a protector such as 'The Acme Mustache Guard' or similar, in silver or gold. Engraved with your initials, as a gift, this is a delicate attention from a lady.

To keep the moustache stiff at night, a moustache net is advisable.

It's the Stropping that Counts

Now that barbers do not call in daily, the modern man must shave himself.

A jolly good scrub with 'Lifebuoy' soap will prepare his skin, followed by the profuse application of lather from a proprietory shaving soap, using a badger hair brush.

The fine feel of a well-shaved chin is best achieved with a good quality cut-throat razor. Sets are available engraved with the owner's name and family crest if desired.

To achieve adequate bite, a blade must be heartily stropped on leather. Any gentleman who

lacks the convenience of a valet should check with his barber to ensure that his stropping technique is adequate, and regularly oil the strop.

Safety razors often come with automatic stropping machines, together with sets of changeable blades marked with each day

of the week, since a blade must be rested between use.

After shaving, the light application of cologne is acceptable, bearing in mind the dictum that a gentleman should smell of nothing but fresh air.

Good grooming concludes with the liberal application to the hair of macassar oil or

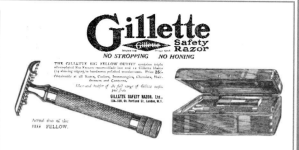

similar to give the hair the desired sleekness. Preparations are available to nourish the hair, cure dandruff, and discreetly colour it to give fading hair additional 'spunk'.

Always Carry Spare Teeth

Brushing teeth with dentifrice powder insures against the ordeal of visiting a dental expert. He never lets you leave without treatment, including silver and mercury fillings, and charges in guineas.

If he fails, assume a genteel solemn expression and rarely smile. In desperate situations, there are some pretty good false sets of teeth made of ivory these days, although it is considered bad form to comment on somebody else's at dinner, unless they openly remove them before eating (a habit entirely reserved for men).

The common habit of twanging the springs attaching the top plate to the mouth should not be derided. Captain Good, hero of Rider Haggard's *King Solomon's Mines* (1885), ingeniously quelled a savage tribe this way.

Always carry spare teeth. As he sunbathed during a cruise, President Grant's false teeth were swept overboard, preventing him from speaking in public when he arrived.

Supporting Roles

The fellow who emits undignified or distressing sounds during sleep should wear a mask in bed. The 'Perfect Breather', with a pouch beneath the nose where one can insert inhaling balm to clear blocked nasal tubes, is accompanied by a pamphlet demonstrating breathing exercises to alleviate the complaint permanently. These will be a double boon, as the man who exercises, before the looking glass, will also breathe new life into his flabby facial muscles.

Rupture sufferers will find their Shangri-La in 'The London Abdominal Supporter', whilst for those chaps suffering deafness,

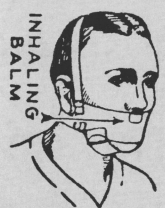

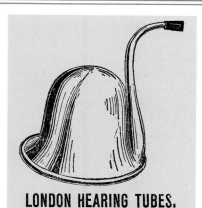

LONDON HEARING TUBES.

**A most useful article for deaf peo-
ple.** Imported by ourselves
No. D2237
Japanned or   Small. Medium. Large.
Nickel plated.. **$3.00 $3.50 $4.00**

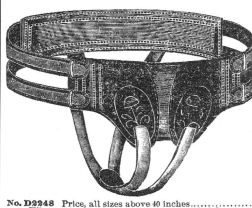

THE LONDON
ABDOMINAL
SUPPORTER,

Well known as
the best and
strongest sup-
porter in the
market. We
guarantee it to be
made from the
finest and stoutest
material that can
be procured, any
part perfect.
No. D2247
Price, all sizes
up to 40 in.. **$1.50**

No. D2248 Price, all sizes above 40 inches.............................. 1.75
When ordering give circumference of abdomen at largest part.

'The London Hearing Tube' will
allow the softest bird twitter to
penetrate the appreciative ear
once more. Those who are shy
of letting others become aware
of their unfortunate affliction
might benefit from Wilson's
'Common Sense Ear Drums',
a new invention scientifically
concealed inside
the ear.

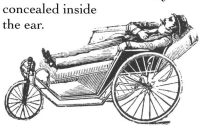

RUPTURE HEALED
Without Pain or Operation
By New, Scientific Invention
TRY IT FREE!

Despite the terrific muscular strain of
bowling and other strenuous sport or
toil, this wonderful discovery safely
retains the rupture and at the same
time heals it. Thousands of men,
women and children report themselves healed of rupture by this
marvellous scientific device. Light,
clean, comfortable, and best of all, so small that it cannot be
noted beneath lightest clothing. Worn night and day with
absolute freedom of movement. Write to day for Free Trial
Offer sent in plain sealed envelope.

BROOKS APPLIANCE CO., LTD.
**(258C) 80, CHANCERY LANE, LONDON, W.C.2.
(258C) 274, DEANSGATE, MANCHESTER.**

A Little Below Par

Gentlemen never suffer from namby-pamby complaints such as migraine. If they feel a twinge, they avoid physicians like the plague. Why pay them five shillings to see you, when a penny compound from the chemist cures everything from heart disease to blood disorders?

Exercise care in buying patent remedies. They might contain arsenic, prussic acid and strychnine. However, since 1899, aspirin has replaced opium in the family medicine chest for general aches and pains.

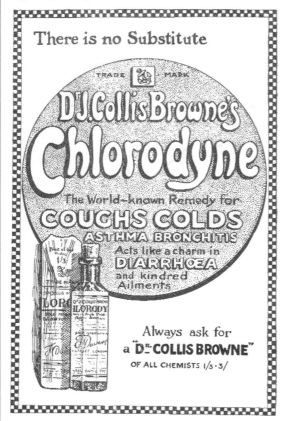

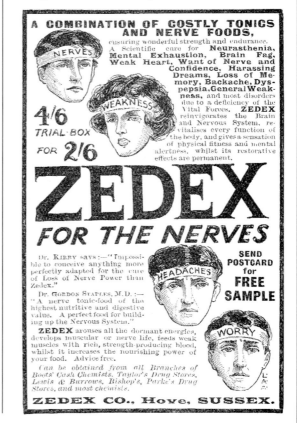

For coughs, diarrhoea and asthma, everybody uses 'Dr Collis Browne's Chlorodyne', a cholera remedy invented by an Indian army surgeon containing chloral, cannabis and two grains of morphia per ounce. In 1892 its makers were prosecuted for not warning of this on the label, however no patent medicine divulges its secrets or the chemist will copy it more cheaply.

Too fond of opium? The St George's Association offers a cure, 'Orphine'. Containing eight

grams of morphine per dose. You are better advised to try that old-fashioned remedy, turtle soup and Turkish baths.

Nerve tonics – pick-me-ups like Hall's 'Coca Wine' – contain cocaine, beloved of flappers and stage door johnnies. Fellows who get hooked end up in Soho's dance-dope clubs where Brilliant Ching, who runs a Chinese restaurant in Regent Street, deals exclusively through pretty women.

HOW TO CURE FEEBLE BLOOD.

If you have a pale face, a sickly pallor, or a washed-out appearance, and are thin, weak, easily tired, prone to melancholy and forebodings, and wish to have a healthy frame, a bright colour to your cheeks, energy, elasticity, and greater capacity to work and endure fatigue, it can be done.

If you suffer from nervous pains and attacks, neuralgia, brain-headache, because the red globules of your blood are run down, deficient in number, weak in quality, so that your whole nervous system is "on an edge," as it were, from want of proper nerve food, "Zotis" Tabules will give the relief you seek.

If you have spots, pimples, eruptions, or impure blood, and a bad complexion, and wish for pure blood, a clear skin, and a soft, bright, smooth complexion, "Zotis" Tabules will do it for you.

If you have Bright's Disease or any other Kidney disorder, causing loss of albumen, sapping the strength, and surely, if slowly, carrying you to the grave, and you wish to have this shocking waste retarded and gradually stopped, "Zotis" Tabules are the remedy you need.

In the *New York Medical Journal*, May 18th, 1889, Professor Austin Flint, M.D., speaks very highly of this tonic saline chalybeate in Bright's Disease and also in Anæmia or Feeble Blood. He states that in only one case out of thirty-five did it fail to cause marked improvement. In all cases the tonic seemed to exert a favourable influence on the quantity of albumen in the water, whilst it acted much more promptly than the remedies usually employed. No unpleasant after effects whatever were produced.

Zotis "Tabules" increase and enrich the red globules of the blood, thereby curing Feeble Blood. This alone can give real and permanent strength, nerve force, and colour to the cheeks. They also disinfect the fluid or liquor of the blood, which drives away impurities and skin eruptions.

SAMPLES FREE ON APPLICATION.
Name "Home Notes."

"ZOTIS" TABULES in boxes, price 1s. 1½d. (post free, 1s. 3d.) ; Six, post paid, for 5s. 6d. ; Twelve, post free, 10s. Sole Proprietors : H. W. SHARP & CO., 28, Gray's Inn Road, London, W.C.

JUST SO! "Just so, just so," says the old gentle-man—"Géraudel's Pastilles—the very thing I want in this beastly weather. Nothing like them for stopping my cough and keeping my lungs right." **JUST SO!**
ALL CHEMISTS SELL THEM. 72 IN A TUBE FOR 1/1½.

A Soldier's Word!

A wounded soldier wrote the other day: "If people only knew the good that Hall's Wine does, everybody would be taking it."

The very strongest of us needs some reinforcement for our strength under the burdens of anxiety and strain we bear to-day.

Hall's Wine gives the very help you need, gives it rightly and pleasantly *without fail*. It has proved a friend to thousands since the war began, bringing strength to those who carry on at home, working marvels for our invalids from the front. Let it help you—from to-day.

A well-known Doctor writes: "It is impossible to take Hall's Wine without being benefited."

Hall's Wine
The Supreme Restorative

GUARANTEE.—Buy a bottle of Hall's Wine to-day. If, after taking half, you feel no real benefit, return us the half-empty bottle, and we will refund your entire outlay.

Large Size, 3s. 6d. Of Wine Merchants, and Grocers & Chemists with Wine licences.

STEPHEN SMITH & CO., LTD., BOW, LONDON.

An Athletic Form

It is not enough for a gentleman to be properly dressed. Beneath, there must be the body of an athlete.

Healthy and hygienic habits are learnt at public school. Any decent man will bound out of bed and perform physical jerks.

Gladiatorial muscles, a slim waist and legs of steel are achieved through regular

WHITELEY EXERCISERS.

The Whitely Exerciser consists of a pure gum cable, of many strands, covered to protect it from the weather, with adjustable handles and swiveled attachments, running over three absolutely noiseless and adjustable cone bearing pulleys so arranged as to be readily suspended in various positions on small hooks attached to door jam, window casing or other convenient wood work, or to hinges on door, (Can easily carry in satchel.)  Can be put up in two minutes, without the aid of a tool of any kind. Can be removed from the hooks and put out of sight in a moment and re-adjusted for use just as quickly. The hooks are of steel wire, strong though small, The workings of Exercise are absolutely noiseless. No straps to buckle. No weights to change. Resistance self-adjusting. No jerks. No dead weights. Evercises all the muscles of the body. All parts warranted. For home use this exerciser is far superior to the chest weights and other cumbrous machines which cost much more money. Order No. 81140½.
No. 1 quality complete with cone-bearing pulleys, etc. Price,..................................$2.95
No. 0 quality, same style but not so well finished. Price....................................$1.85

COMMON SENSE EXERCISERS.

No. 81140¾ Our New Common Sense Exerciser, made of heavy elastic cord, the latest and cheapest exerciser yet produced, can be put up in any part of the room. Our price, complete.................$0.75

scientific exercise. At the gymnasium, men should practise lifting weights: kettle bells, dumbbells or a fine set of barbells. Vary the

activity with Swedish drill or tossing a heavy leather medicine ball, with an invigorating cold shower to finish.

If your club does not boast a gymnasium, a home exercise system such as the 'Charles Atlas' body-building programme will repay your investment tenfold.

A favourite clubmen's game is to swing the length of the swimming pool on overhead rings, wearing evening dress. Ensure that friends have not looped the last ring out of sight, leaving one to fall in.

A suntan is an asset to health. Since Clark Gable removed his shirt in the film *It Happened One Night* (1934), men are bare-chested without censure on beaches.

To promote vigour, wear a ventilated rubber suspensory belt beneath the knickers at all times. To cleanse, have your man boil it regularly.

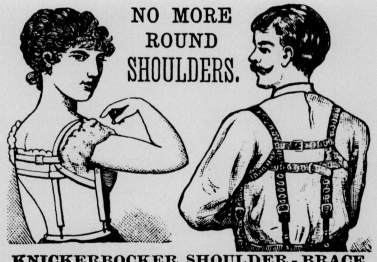

NO MORE ROUND SHOULDERS.

KNICKERBOCKER SHOULDER - BRACE
And Suspender Combined.
Sold by Druggists and General Stores, or sent, post-paid, on receipt of **$1** per pair, plain, or **$1.50** silk-faced. Send chest-measure around the body. Address
KNICKERBOCKER BRACE CO.,
N. A. JOHNSON, Prop'r.   **EASTON, PA.**

The Gentleman's Undergarments

Since its introduction in 1928, the Rayon Union Suit, a set of underwear which never needed taking off (one could shower whilst wearing it) has proved a passing fad. Some chaps wear no underclothing during the summer months, although this causes considerable strain on their suits.

They should investigate sanitary systems which regulate the body temperature by allowing moisture to evaporate, such as Aertex Cellular. Dr Jaeger's woollens were used by Captain Scott on his great Polar expedition, but we are unable to secure his opinion on the subject, as the gentleman has not returned at present.

When choosing, be precise in naming which garment one requires. 'Pants' are ankle- or calf-length, longer than knee-length 'drawers'. 'Knicker-drawers' or 'trunks' are shortest. Specify elastic at the waist, rather than string ties.

'Combinations' or 'long-johns' – one garment functioning as vest and pants – remain a favourite, especially in llama wool. Younger men favour a new 'Y-front' cotton underpant from Coopers of Kenosha in America.

Fast young men wear artificial silk in colours such as salmon pink, previously thought to be effeminate.

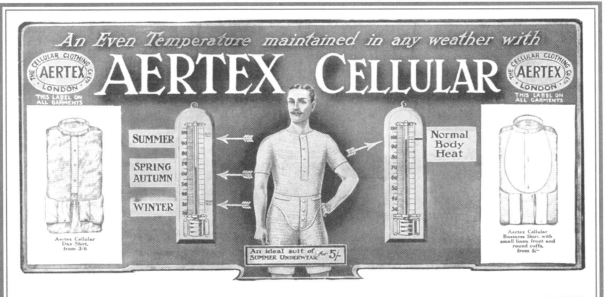

An Even Temperature maintained in any weather with

AERTEX CELLULAR

THE CELLULAR CLOTHING Cº
AERTEX
LONDON
THIS LABEL ON ALL GARMENTS

THE CELLULAR CLOTHING Cº
AERTEX
LONDON
THIS LABEL ON ALL GARMENTS

SUMMER

SPRING AUTUMN

WINTER

Normal Body Heat

Aertex Cellular Day Shirt, from 3/6

Aertex Cellular Business Shirt, with small linen front and round cuffs, from 5/-

An ideal suit of SUMMER UNDERWEAR for 5/-

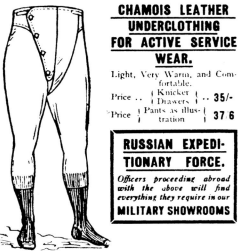

CHAMOIS LEATHER UNDERCLOTHING FOR ACTIVE SERVICE WEAR.

Light, Very Warm, and Comfortable.

Price .. { Knicker Drawers } .. 35/-

Price { Pants as illustration } 37/6

RUSSIAN EXPEDITIONARY FORCE.

Officers proceeding abroad with the above will find everything they require in our MILITARY SHOWROOMS

Hose Supporters.

No. 83185 Hose Supporters. Consists of a belt to go around the waist, with elastic straps, with patent fastenings to attach to the hose to hold them smoothly in their place. They are adjustable to waist and length of limb. State size of waist when ordering. Per pair.....................$0.25

No. 83186 Shoulder Stocking Supporter. An article that meets the popular demand of wheelmen. These supporters do away with elastic bands which bind upon the limbs, causing numbness or swollen veins. Adjustable for any size person. Price, per pair.....................$0.25

No. 83187 Morton's Supporters. Made of best quality Canton flannel. Cool and pleasant to wear. The best fitting and most effective supporter made. Be sure and give waist measurement. Price, per pair.....................$0.25

No. 83187

The Old School Tie

Choosing a necktie is a sacred task, never delegated, least of all to a lady. It is a man's opportunity to express his sentimentality, stopping short of bright red or pink, of course. One bolt of silk makes three narrow ties, so a gentleman orders one tie with a wallet and handkerchief from the remainder.

The ready-knotted tie is vulgar. A knowledge of the hundred recognised tie knots is desirable, but before adopting the Gordion cravat knot, first ensure that your

valet is on hand to cut you free before retiring to bed.

A wardrobe contains ties for lounge suits, including old school, 'Varsity, regimental and club ties, narrow for mornings and wider for afternoons; cravats for frock coats; black bow ties for dinner jackets, white ones for dress coats; and a bow tie for frivolous days, worn with a boater.

Only the most powerful can wear mono-grammed pins instead of ties. But tie-pins, clipping the tie to the shirt, are 'not quite',

unlike collar-pins, which raise the tie knot. George V pulled silk squares through a ring secured with a jewelled horseshoe.

Americans think that the Prince of Wales wears 'God's tie'. They misunderstand his accent. He wears a Guards Tie.

Shape 66

Summit Collars

Quarter size

"*Alone in their excellence*"

AUSTIN REED LTD.

London, Birmingham, Manchester, Liverpool, Leeds, Sheffield, Bristol & Preston

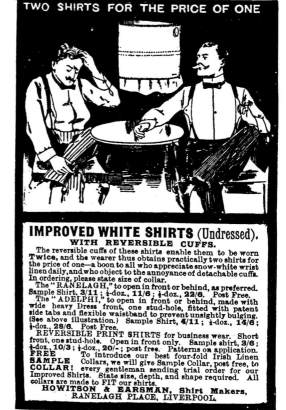

TWO SHIRTS FOR THE PRICE OF ONE

IMPROVED WHITE SHIRTS (Undressed).
WITH REVERSIBLE CUFFS.

The reversible cuffs of these shirts enable them to be worn **Twice**, and the wearer thus obtains practically two shirts for the price of one—a boon to all who appreciate snow-white wrist linen daily, and who object to the annoyance of detachable cuffs. In ordering, please state size of collar.

The "RANELAGH," to open in front or behind, as preferred. Sample Shirt, 3/11 ; ½-doz., 11/6 ; ¾-doz., 22/6. Post Free.

The "ADELPHI," to open in front or behind, made with wide heavy Dress front, one stud-hole, fitted with patent side tabs and flexible waistband to prevent unsightly bulging. (See above illustration.) Sample Shirt, 4/11 ; ½-doz., 14/6 ; ¾-doz., 28/6. Post Free.

REVERSIBLE PRINT SHIRTS for business wear. Short front, one stud-hole. Open in front only. Sample shirt, 3/6 ; ½-doz., 10/3 ; ¾-doz., 20/- ; post free. Patterns on application.

FREE SAMPLE COLLAR! To introduce our best four-fold Irish Linen Collars, we will give Sample Collar, post free, to every gentleman sending trial order for our Improved Shirts. State size, depth, and shape required. All collars are made to FIT our shirts.

HOWITSON & EARSMAN, Shirt Makers, RANELAGH PLACE, LIVERPOOL.

Perfectly Pressed

Trousers have receded from the heights – or should we say widths – of absurdity, the 32-inch leg Oxford Bag worn by 'Varsity men in 1926. A more laudable fashion is the turn-up or cuff, initiated when the Prince of Wales rolled up his trousers for a muddy walk to Ascot's stables. He forgot to unroll them. Others found the idea was excellent rain protection. If anyone asks why your trousers are turned up, a good joke is to reply, 'Because it's raining in London', even if you are in Monte Carlo.

The Prince has also made front trouser-creases quite 'the thing' after he tore his trousers on the mudguard of a car and bought a ready-made pair in a shop, creased from storage.

A gentleman never has a large wardrobe; that would prevent him looking modish. Yet trousers, most particularly, should never look new. Your butler should wear them in. Your driver should don your jackets in the rain.

No. 83188 Ostergren's Patent Trouser Guard, a neat and handy device for saving the pants from dirt and grease; can be carried in the vest pocket or worn around the legs under the pants when not in use.
Price, per pair **$0.05**
No. 83190 **The Perfection Trouser Guard,** made of finest spring steel, to wear around ankle, same as Ostergren's.
Our special price, per pair................... **$0.03**
Per dozen.......... .... **.35**

THE ONLY REMEDY FOR BAGGY KNEES.

THE ENORMOUS SALE THIS INVENTION COMMANDS IS THE BEST TEST OF ITS MERITS.

IMPORTANT,
Avoid imitations, and insist upon JOHN HAMILTON & CO.'S PATENT, each of which is stamped with Name and Trade Mark.

If any difficulty in obtaining, or other Stretchers are attempted to be substituted, send P.O.O. (with 6d. extra for carriage) to the Makers, 7, PHILIP LANE, LONDON, E.C.

JOHN HAMILTON & CO.'S TROUSERS STRETCHER

P R I C E S.
Polished Walnut Clamps, Nickel Rod and Fittings 8/6
Polished Birch Clamps, Bronze ditto 4/-
Plain Ditto ditto ditto 3/6
Plain Birch Clamps, Rod not jointed 2/6

OF ALL TAILORS AND HOSIERS.

The 'Patent Adjustable Brace' (with crosstree at the back) is ideal anchorage for trousers worn high up the waist. Those favouring a more casual effect will wear belts, made easier now that tailors have added 'waist bands' with belt carriers.

Hat Tricks

Silk top hats are not meant to be practical. They are a badge of good breeding. On the *Titanic*, Benjamin Guggenheim exhorted the men to wear tailcoats and top hats so that 'at least we shall die like proper gentlemen'.

The top hat is a tool to convey its wearer's exact feelings for others without the vulgarity of speech. For a cold formality, lightly touch the brim then tilt the hat slowly over the eyes. Whilst riding, you lift the hat straight up then tilt it abruptly to the right. But for the Greeting Jovial, doff the hat and wave it. For a lady, place it over your heart with a flourish. Never ask a man wearing a tilted top hat where he is going. He is clearly on some private mission.

Top hats are always worn at the races and at balls, except when waltzing, when the hat reserves one's partner's chair. At the theatre, Mr Gibus's folding top hat, which clips into the brim, is a courtesy allowing others to see the stage. Young bloods prefer Mr Kriegk's horizontally folding top hat, available since 1912.

Any man over 25 wears roomy leather gloves and carries a cane. In town, dark, spotted malacca with a crystal pommel at the top and a silver-tipped ebony stick for evenings. Country canes have a rougher feel, with a silver handle representing a horse or dog.

Suits You Sir!

Suits are not designed. They are bespoke, ordered during discussion with one's tailor. Begin by choosing the fabric, rather than the cut, and end by fixing a date for trying-on. (Never 'fitting'.)

The tailor is your secret, one of the few to see you in your underclothes. (Few men, that is!) Don't give his name out willy-nilly; but as a great favour. However, Hollywood actors, who wear their own wardrobe on film sets, openly patronise Savile Row: Fred Astaire to Anderson & Sheppard, Cary Grant to Kilgour and Clark Gable to Henry Poole.

The idea that a gentleman's suit should be unobtrusive, went after the dancer-singer Jack Buchanan wore a new cut to America. Now it's hard to get in to your tailors since Savile Row is full of Americans trying to copy him. It had wide lapels, padded shoulders and tapered trousers. Scholte's, the military tailor patronised by the Prince of Wales, uses uniform-cutting tricks to make

ordinary men look taller and stronger, giving them an air of authority in a crisis – exactly what the Americans need after the Wall Street Crash of 1929.

If you can't get to Savile Row, cut along to Austin Reed in Regent Street for passable ready-made suits. Out of funds? Well, walk tall with built-up shoes.

Heirs and Graces

Little gentlemen never raise their voices. Nor their kilts when quite properly wearing no underwear – as four year-old Lord Claud Hamilton did to Queen Victoria. Instead of bowing, he stood on his head in his kilt, an accomplishment of which he was very proud. Expressing deep penitence, he was taken back to make his apologies, when he did precisely the same thing over again. Didn't stop him becoming a courtier later, as his brother Frederick tells the story.

Until they reach two, boys are called 'the child' rather than by their names, in case something happens to them. Should any show a tendency to protruding ears, it is wise to make them wear an ear cap in the nursery and during the night.

Tiny boys wear frilly robes and flowing curls. They graduate with a hair-cut at Truefitt's, to wearing patriotic sailor suits, velvet Little Lord Fauntleroy breeches or Highland dress, in deference to our beloved Royal Family's love of Balmoral in the Highlands. Norfolk suits with plus-fours are the best wear for a boy. Eton suits should not be worn unless a boy actually attends Eton.

Boys need an education. Except the eldest, who will inherit the family estate. He just needs all the money. Spare sons have to bite the bullet and support themselves in the Professions, the Church or the Army. Or politics.

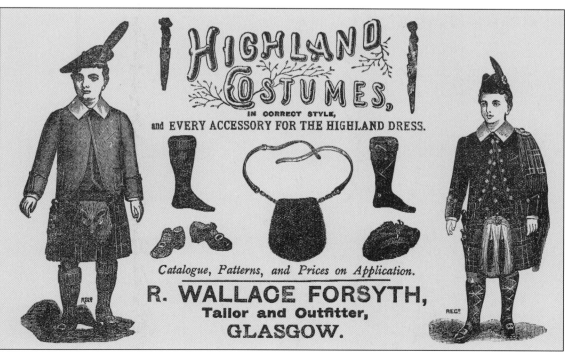

Fine Footwear

Never trust a chap with fancy footwear. Take the Prince of Wales. Brown shoes – or worse, banana-coloured. Stepping off the ship in America wearing suede like some nancy-boy. Looks fast. Fringed-tongue brogues. Two-toned, with white, worn off the golf course!

Co-respondent shoes they call them in the gentlemen's clubs.

You can't put a foot wrong in Lobb's hand-made boots polished to match your carriage. Ruinously expensive, but there you are. Or plain Oxford black patent leather shoes. Your valet must make a good job of washing and ironing the laces and polishing the black soles. If it makes them slippery, no matter. A

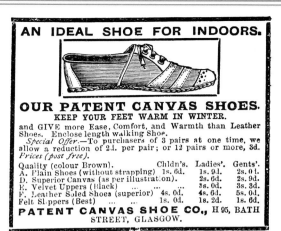
gentleman never walks over fifty paces, the
proper distance between home and stables.

Did you hear about that tailor sacked for
refusing to wear spats? He sued, but lost on
the grounds that his improper dress sullied
his employer's reputation.

D——d nuisance, spats, if buttoned too
tight over your socks and suspenders, but
necessary in polite society. They hide your

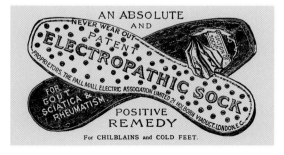

socks, which are virtually camouflaged
anyway by matching your trousers!

In the evening, squeeze the feet into black
patent pumps and embroidered silk stock-
ings. Whistler, a painter chappie, fancied
himself, wore pink bows on his pumps.
Another bounder. It's all in the shoes.

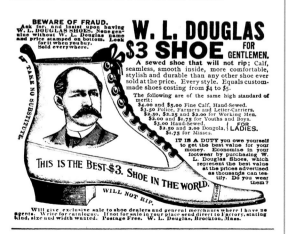

The Gentleman's Necessities

Men dislike carrying bags. Their pockets hold all life's daily necessities.

In the jacket breast pocket, a cologne-scented white cotton handkerchief with hand-rolled border is useful. If snuff is taken from a pocket snuff-box, the handkerchief should be brown to hide the tobacco stains.

Bounders carry gimmicks like the speckerchief, an eyeglass case disguised as a

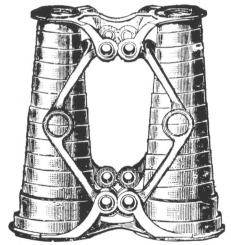

Instantly Opened and Focussed

Instantly Closed for Pocket.

handkerchief, or the Amore, advertised as 'a distinctive idea for every man of derring-do' bearing printed lipstick smudges.

The waistcoat pocket conceals a gold-rimmed monocle on a black ribbon for occasional reading. If a pocket watch is kept there, a chain across the stomach is 'not quite'. Wrist watches are a convenient innovation for officers who need their hands free.

A fruit knife, the blade folding into the handle, is carried even to dinner parties. Fountain pens have replaced pen-knives now that quills are no longer a necessity.

A pocket book for making notes and a calling-card case are essential. The wallet contains fresh Bank of England notes, but these are used only to pay betting debts and restaurant bills, as most establishments offer monthly accounts. Although useful abroad, a pocket revolver is not normally carried in England.

'STRAND' WATCH with Cap on.
ALL ENGLISH— Silver, £5 ; 18-ct. Gold, £13 15s. Special Size for Ladies, £5 15s. and £12 15s.

Inclement Weather

In inclement weather, carry a black silk umbrella. But only use it to hail a cab when it is raining. Never open it except to have the silk renewed when it has perished.

Oilskin coats, rubber macintoshes and even greatcoats are less convenient than Thomas Burberry's rainproof gaberdines, made especially for sportsmen. As the advertisements proclaim, they are 'Proof against the Heaviest Rains and Mists, the Stoutest Thorn or Fishhook'. They can be repeatedly repaired, as is demonstrated by an enthusiast who wrote to Burberry: "You made me a rain-proof coat in 1911. Twenty years later, I still use it when tiger-shooting in the jungles, in boats when shooting crocodiles, beside car and ordinary wear."

The Army's trenchcoat, ordered from Burberry by the Government for the Great War, is to be worn in *Casablanca* by Humphrey Bogart. We hope he won't find it rather warm.

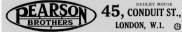

Sleep Attire

Whilst some believe that any garment worn
in bed is improper, pyjamas are generally
accepted as the modern, healthy alternative
to nightgowns. Introduced by colonialists,
they have been made popular by actors
adopting them as decent attire during
bedroom scenes, although sensitive ladies
have been known to leave the theatre.

You can buy pyjamas by the dozen.
You will find them near the silk tie, handkerchief and waistcoat departments in a
gentlemen's outfitter such as Gorringes.
They are brighter-hued than day
clothes, because their colours allow a
man to express a private, softer side
of his nature. If he chooses stripes,

Herr Freud might say that it signified a secret wish to be a tiger in the privacy of the bedroom.

Even if a man preens himself in the privacy of his dressing-room, remember: peacocks don't wear canary yellow pyjamas. They might expose him to ridicule during country-house weekends if, by mischance, he enters the wrong room. As one chap did, leaping onto the Bishop of Bath and Wells' bed with the cry of 'Cock a doodle doo!'

A silk dressing gown, doubling as a smoking jacket, is essential to the lounging, lazy mornings beloved of bachelors.

The Finest Tobacco

Smoking stiffens the upper lip. A briar pipe clamped between the teeth is an excellent reason for rarely speaking, a very gentlemanly trait.

Cigarettes, introduced by soldiers in 1900, have become essential. A correctly stocked table-box carries Virginia on one side, Turkish or Egyptian Ovals on the other. Gentlemen's cigarettes sport their initials, crest and colour, making it hard for any bounder to replenish his private cigarette case from his host's supply. By the way, you never read the dedication engraved inside a personal cigarette case – as socially dangerous as commenting on family likenesses in children.

After dinner, you take your host's Havana cigar and use your own cigar-cutter and

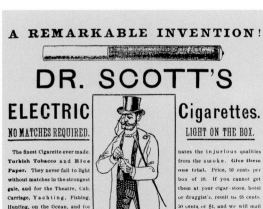

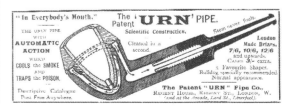

portable ashtray. Serious smokers retire to the smoking room, donning a smoking-jacket to protect the dress shirt. No need for matches with the automatic lighter, invented by Alfred Dunhill in 1924, at the request of a wounded officer with one arm. Or try self-lighting cigarettes, with a built-in match tip to strike on any surface.

If your appetite for Three Nuns is getting on top of you, send for Sears & Roebuck's Sure Cure for the Tobacco Habit, 'also one of the best tonics for sexual weakness ever made.'

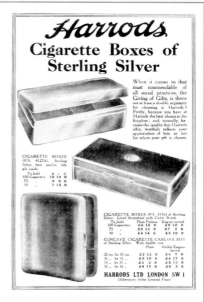

Indoor Pursuits

The family gathered round the hearth gazes with shining eyes at Papa ready to instruct and entertain them, perhaps with a new table-top Ping Pong game bought from Hamley's toy emporium.

A man who does conjuring tricks is a god to his wife and family. Manuals and aids can

be purchased in advance. That popular publication *Diversions & Pastimes* describes other amusing family games such as leaving someone to hold a glass of water to the ceiling with a walking stick, then using a stop-watch to time how long they keep their temper.

During winter evenings, children will enjoy mathematical puzzles or games with paper and string before bed. Then, while his wife

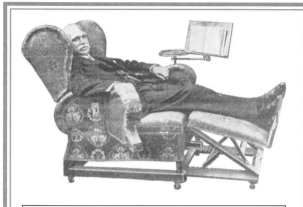

reads a three-volume novel from the lending library, a gentleman settles into his armchair and studies *The Times*, or perhaps skims *Punch* magazine for some article of interest such as 'The Romance of the Battle-Cry'.

Many men read the Pink 'Un, as the *Sporting Times* is known. He will take the precaution of locking this inside his desk, as it contains off-colour humour. What is necessary for him to know, is decidedly improper for ladies.

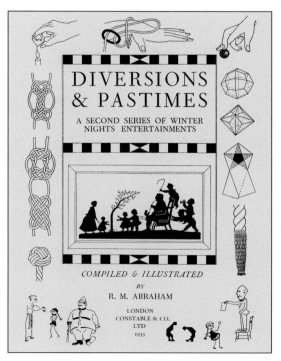

Musical Interludes

If your wife cannot play the piano, you might send for a correspondence course ('They laughed when I sat down at the piano . . . but when I started to play.'). Hopeless cases should purchase a pianola which, worked with the feet, gives the illusion of play by the person at the keyboard.

Those who must dance have gramophones playing popular jazz such as 'I can't dance cos I've got ants in my pants' or 'You're the polar bear's pyjamas'. The reflective music-

lover will prize two melancholy melodies from Columbia Records, 'The Emigrant' and 'The Nightingale', sung by Miss Dora Labette to an orchestra obbligato.

A gentleman knows how to play the piano-accordian but never inflicts his knowledge on others. However, the ability to render popular ballads such as 'Sonny Boy' on the banjo is a useful accomplishment during boating parties or if fulfilling a social duty by performing at charity concerts. Music-hall ditties entitled 'We must all frou-frou till we can't frou-frou anymore' or similar are not respectably sung in public.

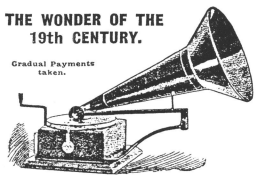

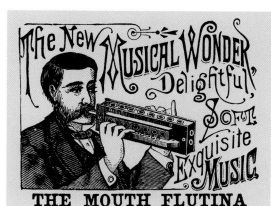

If a music-lover is of a practical bent, and can carve fretwork, the *Hobbies Handbook* shows him how to make other interesting instruments from the mandolin to the phono-fiddle.

Club Life

Boodle's for gamblers, The Garrick for thespians, the Junior Constitutional for politicians . . . A chap's club is a male-only haven allowing like-minded fellows to do the things they aren't allowed to do at home. Clubs have foibles. The Pelican once cooked the club parrot for an unsuspecting member who rudely demanded 'a bird' when game was out of season.

The Bachelors', the model for Bertie Wooster's Drones Club, allows women inside, but fines members £25 upon marriage.

To be black-balled – refused membership – is the ultimate embarrassment. You might be discreetly advised to withdraw beforehand, as Oscar Wilde was – twice.

Let's slip off to a night-club. What about the Grafton Galleries, where we can do the Black Bottom or Charleston while the band plays 'I'm Just Wild About Harry'? It's not

serious sin. The nude drawings for sale are covered with tissue paper during the day and we'll drink Turk's Blood, made of fruit juice, with sandwiches and iced cakes from Gunter's, the Berkeley Square pastry shop.

Not for ladies are other less select clubs like the Bat or Uncle's. If you wear correct evening dress, the head waiter will instantly propose you for membership, seconded by the doorman.

Teeing-off

Did you see today's newspaper? Pictures of the Prince of Wales captaining himself in at the Royal and Ancient Golf Club in St Andrews. Instead of a Norfolk jacket, he wore a 'sweater', they called it. Knitted. Noisy colours. If it spreads, the caddies will lose respect.

This sweater looked like those knitted yellow waistcoats chaps took a fancy to, after the War. The things women knitted

to cheer up the returning heroes. But they say the Prince knitted this

sweater himself! Some fellows at my club saw him doing *petit point* embroidery at that weekend place of his, the Fort, but I don't believe that is how a man occupies himself in 1922.

At least he has found nothing to replace the tweed cap and good old Plus Fours. That American chappy, who played a round at the Club yesterday, wondered why we don't call them knickerbockers as they do. I set him straight. We British lengthened them four inches, so Plus Fours it is. More comfortable and gives you something to tuck your long white socks into. The Prince wears Plus Eights. What next, coloured socks to match the sweater? Mark my words, his game will suffer.

Hunting, Shooting and Fishing

Indoor activities exist merely to fill the time when it rains too heavily for sport outdoors. At country house parties, the shooting of game birds will rightly dominate the conversation from dawn till dinner, with the addition of deer stalking in rougher terrain.

Stout Norfolk tweeds with horn-buttons, deerstalker hats and sturdy footwear strike the right note for the primary sports of hunting, shooting and fishing. Game-keepers wear bowlers. Duck shooters will appreciate the convenience of a grass suit.

GRASS SUITS.

No. 8673. For wild goose, duck and all kinds of shore bird shooting; made of long tough marsh grass into cape coat with hood. Weigh less than four pounds, are convenient to wear and shoot from. Make good waterproofs in rainy weather, are easily packed and carried. Hunters appreciate the value of these suits, as no blind or bough house is necessary when shooting on marshes. Single suits, each................ ....$1.75

For the ceremony of riding to hounds, club colours are worn, be they hunting pinks, blue or green. The coat is set off by moleskin breeches, silk top hat, boots with turned-out border and leather gloves. Choosing a waistcoat is always left to last. In the country, it is worn longer than for town, and embroidered by certain fair fingers eagerly awaiting the huntsman's return.

Commodious country-houses boast a 'men's wing' with smoking-room, billiard table and sports tackle rooms

together. This enables fellows to retire after the port and admire the host's fine collection of 'Perfect' rods by Hardy Brothers, together with trophies.

In the absence of decent hunting, riding or walking is superior to loitering by the fireside in tigerskin slippers.

Play up and Play the Game

Good chaps don't sit swotting, but go out on the playing fields and make a decent fist of cricket, rugby football, football and tennis. They play for dear old school, aim to be

FOR POPULARITY...
always keep those social engagements!

ELLIMAN'S
liminates pain
EMBROCATION

BOTTLES 1/1½ 2/9 & 4/-
JARS 11/- & 22/-
Prepared only by
ELLIMAN Sons & Co.
Slough
ENGLAND

capped at 'Varsity – and if not playing for Country, at least turn out for the country-house Gentlemen's team. Games are no respecters of social distinction, although the Village team are served their tea separately. They prefer it.

Identical clothes, especially casual sports jackets, are generally worn by players and spectators these

days. For football and boating, one can order a tolerable home-knit jersey with long sleeves and in the right colour stripes, at the Army and Navy Stores. You can be sure of getting the right kit for all 34 sports at Lillywhites, the University of Sports in Piccadilly. If you have left it out of its press for too long, they will restring your tennis racket too.

During the winter months, the Alpine air will soon blow the cobwebs away. Mountaineering,

skating and tobogganing are popular, but skiing reigns supreme. Those awfully jolly hand-knitted turtle-neck jumpers with matching caps are no longer considered 'fast' on the slopes, and you can keep them on during tea dances in the afternoons.

Only a cad does not allow a lady to win at croquet or badminton.

Evening Engagements

Evening dress must be worn when going out at night, even to the Tivoli Music-Hall for a certain chorus-girl's performance of that notorious song, 'Rumpty-tiddley-umpty-ay'.

If going on for a bite at Simpson's-on-the-Strand or Rules, correct dress will ensure that you are not given a table 'in Siberia' the term for those far from the social lions such as Mr Winston Churchill or the Aga Khan.

Where no ladies are present, at a Grill Room for instance, you can wear the new informal dinner jacket with black tie and soft collar. But in a dress coat – midnight blue, which looks more black than black – the stiff wing collar should be fastened with collar studs. Eschew the temptation to 'cut corners' with rubber collars, strap-on dickey fronts or paper cuff-covers and *never* wear a white handkerchief or scarf. Before donning a coat or cape, a chest

SAVOY HOTEL - LONDON
GRAND FOYER & RESTAURANT

protector worn over the shirt front will preserve its pristine state.

Although Fabergé enamel buttons have enjoyed a vogue, jewellery is vulgar. Pearl white studs should fasten the shirt front; gold cufflinks the cuffs.

The buttonhole orchid stays fresh all night if you tape it inside a tiny vase of water behind the lapel.

Sea Air and Bathing

When the sun has got his hat on, we wear our panama on the Pullman to Brighton. We take a hip flask, but no opera glasses. Cads use these to spy on ladies bathing. However, we keep a penny for 'What the Butler Saw', the slot machine at the end of the pier.

Gentlemen bathe separately from ladies. In case any are tempted to skip church and bathe on Sundays, ladies sit on the beach reading prayer books. This position affords an excellent view of chaps rising from the sea naked – the only manly way to conquer Britannia's waves.

Calecons – string-waisted bathing trunks – have been available since 1860 but cling to the extremities when wet. 'A boy brought to the [bathing] machine door, two towels as I thought, but when I came out of the water, I found that one was a pair of short red and white striped drawers,' writes a respectable

Bailey's Swimming Glove.
LIKE A DUCK'S FOOT.

Learn to swim, to float, to become in water as expert as a **DUCK** by using Bailey's Rubber Swimming Glove. They are made of Pure Para Rubber, which makes a web between the fingers like a duck's foot, doubling the power of the stroke, and greatly increasing the speed, ease, and pleasure of swimming.

Men's, $2; Women's, $1.75; Children's, $1.50 Pair.

Sent postage paid on receipt of price.

C. J. BAILEY & CO.,
Everything in Rubber Goods.

THE terms include golf, tennis, croquet, bowls, squash, badminton, swimming, dancing, cinema and entertainments. So you're bound to have a pretty good time when you come down for the Autumn Season.

N.B. — The Brown-Smiths were disappointed last year. They thought they needn't book in advance.

curate, Francis Kilvert. 'Unaccustomed to such things, I had bathed naked and scandalised the beach. The young ladies strolling nearby seemed to have no objection.'

Some chaps wear the one-piece University Costume used during Oxbridge swimming competitions. Now it has decorous sleeves and legs and has become a decent woollen costume – as exciting as a soggy doggy when wet.

Out for a Spin

Taking one's lady friend out for a spin with the Cycling Club? These new Rover 'Safety Cycles' are absolute pippins for touring. I see you've fitted your machine with Harrison's Patent Alarm Bell, which rings continuously. Silly law, demanding that you warn carriage-drivers of your approach.

Only bounders and scorchers wear knitted woollen cycling sweaters. But knicker-

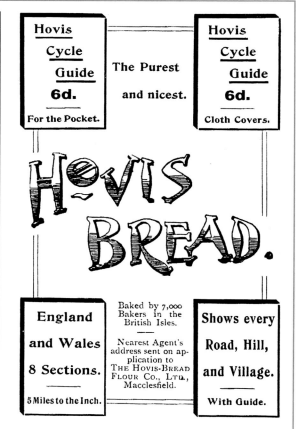

bockers won't get caught in the pedals as trousers would, and Norfolk jackets of pepper and salt tweed are snug – though don't take a tip from Lord Granville Gordon, who shocked London society by happily cycling down Pall Mall wearing his deer-stalking tweeds.

BICYCLE SUITS

$2·95 $3·50 $4·50 $5·50

$3·25 $375 $4·75 $6·00

Our line of Bicycle Clothing is very extensive,

We have made arrangments with one of the largest man-ufacturers of Bicycle Clothing in America to supply us, and for the coming season we can offer you such bargains as were never offered before. The great craze for bicycles has induced one of the largest clothing manufacturers in America to turn his attention to the manufacture of bicycle clothing exclusively and he has gotten out a line that is without an equal in the market, and under our arrangments we are prepared to furnish you these goods at less money than your local dealer can buy them in large quantities. Our bicycle suits are all fine tailor made throughout, cut on the latest style patterns by expert cutters to fit perfectly; they are elegantly trimmed and finished, and in every way they make a first class suit.

RULES FOR MEASUREMENT. Measurements should be taken exactly the same as for other suits. See our "Rules for Measurement" on another page

OUR SPECIAL TERMS. Bicycle Suits, like all other clothing, will be sent C. O. D. by express, subject to examination, on receipt of **$1.00 as a guarantee of good faith.** You can examine the suit at the express office, and if found perfectly satisfactory and exactly as represented, pay the express agent the balance and express charges and the suit is yours. Three per cent discount allowed if cash in full accompanies your order.

No. 4579   OUR $2.95 BICYCLE SUIT. This suit is made of a light tan diagonal suiting, good wearing goods and consists of one bicycle coat and one pair of bicycle pants. Coat is made with 4 buttons, sack style. It is the best bicycle suit for the money that has been offered.

Price...$2.95
Separate Bicycle Pants Only, price $1.50
Bicycle Cap to match, price....................................0.35
No. 4580   MENS' DARK OXFORD MIXED BICYCLE SUITS. This is a very firmly woven fabric and will give first-class service.

The Open Road

Is that your new *teuf-teuf*? How spiffing! Haven't you heard that word? Means automobile. It's French. We all use it.

I should stock up with Motor Car Spirit when you get the chance. Hard to find. A firm called Carless (ha! ha!) sells superior stuff called Petrol. And with roads as they are, full of horseshoe nails, carry spare pneumatic tyres too.

Take my furrier's name. That loose duster coat is all very well for summer, but with open-topped cars in winter, you need a snug leather coat with a beaver lining and Persian lamb collar.

All gentlemen drive fast: up to 30 miles per hour. Buy a vibration-

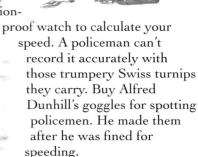

proof watch to calculate your speed. A policeman can't record it accurately with those trumpery Swiss turnips they carry. Buy Alfred Dunhill's goggles for spotting policemen. He made them after he was fined for speeding.

Talking of speeding, join the Automobile Association. Their motor scouts will fail to salute you if there are any speed traps ahead. The police tried to stop

this, but failing to salute isn't illegal, what? The AA served *Queue de Boeuf Thick* as *Police Timing* at its annual dinner to celebrate.

Well, I must *teuf-teuf* off now. See you on the road!

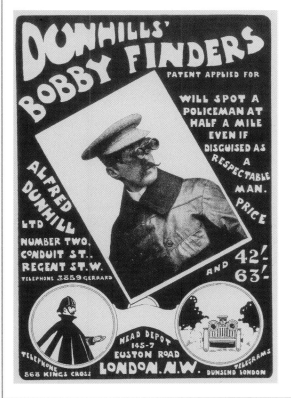

The Gentleman Abroad

The beauty of abroad is, a chap's off the reins. He can do and wear what he fancies as he explores what foreign parts he fancies. White flannel trousers and blue blazer, like Rudolph Valentino. Or a sports jacket with one mother-of-pearl button.

With the Great War over, rivers of champagne connect the best places, from Torquay to Le Touquet, Deauville to Dinard, from Brighton to Buenos Aires, one called London-by-the-sea, the other London over-the-sea.

Pack my trunk with boaters and socks to match the hatbands – black for spring, blue

for summer. A chum is driving his Bugatti from Paris to Monte Carlo. I can join him if I take today's Pullman to Paris. I'll pay my respects to the Folies Bergère tonight – carefully comparing the girls' legs to the

✦ OVER ✦
TO THE
CONTINENT

Holidays on the Continent are so easy to arrange nowadays. The Continental Departments and enquiry offices of the Railway Companies and the Travel Agencies are only too willing to help you to choose your destination and arrange your journey.

AND WHAT A WEALTH OF CHOICE!

Once put the Channel or the North Sea between you and the daily round and the tonic effect of different life and surroundings is immediately felt. Try the golden sands of France or Belgium, the lakes and the blue skies of Italy. Switzerland, land of mountain sunshine. Holland, with its quaint cities and customs, or the scenic beauties of Norway, Sweden and Denmark.

Over this year— to the Continent!

Gaiety Girls' in London. Then perhaps cruise to Brioni, that island everyone's talking about.

I've booked a Thomas Cook trip to Egypt. Now you can fly from Croydon Airport. From Cairo, I might take a flying safari in Kenya with Beryl Markham and Baron Bror Blixen. I've heard the Happy Valley set get up to some tricks out there, what?

ACKNOWLEDGEMENTS

Thoroughly good chaps have been Lesley O'Mara for asking me to scribble my thoughts, and Gabrielle Mander for being a brick about the whole thing.

Archivist and historians are good eggs. Peter Tilley and Marc Burrows of Alfred Dunhill Museum & Archive, 48 Jermyn St, London SW1, by whose kind permission we reproduce the Dunhill advertisements here. John Arlett, Senior Sword Advisor of Wilkinson Sword Limited. David G. Thursby of Burberry's Ltd. Peter Foden, Boots Company Historian. Colin Gammons, The Royal College of Art. The staff of the National Art Library at the V&A Museum. Jessica Talmage of the Mary Evans Picture Library and Professor Lou Taylor of Brighton University.

On the home front, Andy Tribble has been absolutely top hole at initiating me into the many mysteries of manliness. Sue Davies helped find pictures. And cordial halloos to William and Charlie Tribble, tomorrow's gentlemen, for laughing with me.

THE AUTHOR

Each morning, author Jane Furnival removes her earcap, waxes her moustache and hones her figure on dumbbells before sitting down to scribble in her authorial turret in her home, a crumbling gothic chapel in South London. Her husband Tribble gallantly allows her to win at croquet but not to choose his neckties. Heir and spare William and Charlie wear Eton suits on all occasions.

PICTURE CREDITS

Mary Evans Picture Library: Front cover, *left*; p. 9 *below*; p. 11 *top right* and *below left*; p. 60 *right*; Alfred Dunhill Museum & Archive: p. 61 *below left*; Savoy, London, Archives: p. 54 *left*.
Whilst every effort has been made to acknowledge all illustrations, the publishers apologise if the name of any contributor has been omitted.

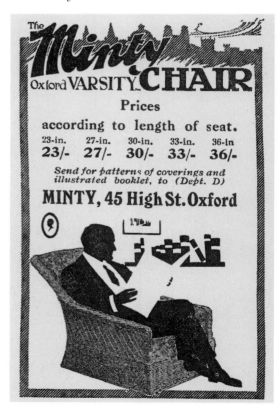